Sunlight On Dew Laden Grass

R.C. Davis

CONTENTS

A HIDDEN PASSAGEWAY

A projecting light deceives, born without intention
false impressions blossom from optical illusion
too many light waves for any lazy eye to count
yet, the door remains

It is simply not what you think it should be
if I tell you it's a door and it doesn't look like a door
you won't believe me until I show you
then—it's a door

To a passageway, a secret, only, until everybody knows
and if forgotten, a secret once more
where shadows rest in empty corners, and slither away from the light
A corridor

A deliciously quiet place within the walls
where you can move without detection
coming to a stop, no one will know
unless you are sharing

What is the use of a hidden passageway?
if no one knows, it is like a tree falling in the woods
it is not the sound that matters
it is knowing that there are, trees

AS A MAN

I cannot wake and go forth
In my day without conviction
Or purpose filled intent
In expressing solemn diction

My submersion into romance
More or less the hopeless version
Should not be misconstrued
As a sign of my defection

For I am only human
Fragility is still my lot
I could choose to embrace you
Or simply choose to not

My quest in seeking beauty
Has become an everyday affair
The context curve of a woman's hip
The dapple in her hair

What I think the color of the wind may be
Or my notice of a spherical stone
The finch upon the veranda rail
Or the old man that sits alone

Tears I shed at subtle metaphor
Children's laughter in the air
A vast expanse of clover field
My inability to just not care

To seek my own divinity
Free from pious clone
For honestly, I know what is right
My choice will be my own

I don't need someone to tell me
The aesthetics of sunlight bold
Across the misty glade
and the grass blade turned to gold

Of the sanctity of innocence
A time we are all allowed
This treasure of our childhood
Shall not be disavowed

To talk with you, one on one
In hopes we may understand
What it simply means to be us
No authority or command

To feel the texture of the entity
Course wet fur or silky kin
The rugged bark of a willow tree
Your soft and subtle skin

So many things a man can feel
If only he would acquiesce
Seize the day whenever you can
for the sake of love, not duress

BECAUSE I CAN ONLY CALL IT TIME

It speaks to me
the light coming up in the world
to reflect and shine on the sparse overcast above the horizon
small, gray dappled clouds, floating
a soft rolling tune, just under our radar
I could easily accept the scientific explanation
just another planet revolving around a sun star entity
but no, there is more…
all, within its light, is energizing
everything within its scope, is day

BLACK MANTA RAY DREAMS, WHERE SLEEP IMPEDES DROWNING

My dreams are fish. Black manta rays emerging from the murk. Slowly flying through my night. Muted and shy. Barely a memory. A time, I can be in the deep without drowning. Where the ocean's version of stars crawl slowly across the sand covered floor. I am only visiting. Riding the sun up from where waves lap the horizon. The real world unfolds before me. A dioxide existence. Forever seeking elusive dream states. So hard to just fall away into stupefaction. That daily arduous journey toward dusk, where the surf murmurs contentment. I surrender at the wall of eroding consciousness.

DAYBREAK

(For Andre Norton)

Find me crouched
upon a single craggy finger
projecting into space

Suspended a mile above
great skeletal ruins of old civilizations
Of peculiar contrast against the bald faced
rock cliff glowing sepia

Cloud picture, fog serpents
writhing against the face of a dawn fracturing sun
A sky sea, painted scarlet
fading to blushing hue
Pierced by the late, departing hawks of a darker hour
Fleeting shadows extinguishing stars in passing
Previous. Dark death on a silent black background

Left alone in this future
on a twenty-third century day
The wooden shaft of my steel tipped lance
smoothed by constant use, until splintered
You knew me once, before you left this place,
for the tomblike quiet of a city scape
Dark, glassless windows to follow your every move
Menacing doorways allow you in for quick termination

You now burden me with a troublesome memory
Eking out my existence
north of the 'blow-up land'
Where the soft breeze laces the fields
with the putrid reminders of what has happened here
If you were to come back,
you would not recognize me
Our portraits fade

THE FLICKERING LIGHT OF A BICYCLE CAR TRAIN RIDE

The gray bench seat in the bicycle car glistens.
Perched upon slick, plastic coating, I'm riding,
riding a south bound German train, the straight-man in a curved world
a bold sun splatters itself through windows without resistance
the motion stops with a lengthy squeal of steel on steel, sparks imagined
the door, sliding, allows the middle-aged, short-skirted mother like woman
onboard from a colorless concrete platform, no one waving
a 'stroboscopic' movie starting over, a brilliant orb jumping
from tree to tree, from tree to pole, buildings come and go
reinforcing my illusion, the outside wheel spinning
a minute of night-like tunnel intermission to rest my eyes, soothing
darkness
speckled with soft white wall lamps to keep it real, then flash! and
we're back
the woman spreads her legs for me, sending an exaggerated wink
she wants to be my leading lady, the ephemeral face in my only scene
I look away—I don't want that—I want the flickering I want just to
ride the inner wheel
to be the star of this rolling zoetrope on predestined rails
there is a comfort that comes with a multi bicycle audience
their cyclophiliacs chatting with levity
I know how I want this story to end

HARDWIRED FOR THE PRIMITIVE

I couldn't live in my dinosaur brain anymore
All the furniture in there was way too 50's
    My overstuffed chair was too shallow
    I could never get comfortable
    The snake skinned lamp too dim
    Shedding, barely enough light on my life

There was a caveman that came to visit sometimes
    He brought his club and always stayed too long
        He liked me when I stayed inside that place
        Clinging to me when I tried to leave
        Trying to convince me that we were related
        A link that no one could put a finger on

I remember the day I didn't go back into that cage for lizards
    I left everything behind, including my ancient music
        I stepped outside, moving into a sunlit place
        Where the windows were clean enough to see out
        With a chair that offered sufficient depth
        Quiet enough for me to truly hear the living/breathing

The caveman tries to call on me sometimes when I least expect
    I make it hard for him, so he might be able to take the hint
        It's not that I will ever forget that small space
        Where unpleasant recall flooded my box
        Making that realm wet with predisposition
        Where a he-man lays sleeping, waiting for my return

I CAN SEE~FINE

I put myself here, paying the price for entry
there was no contestation at the door
turquoise slides penetrate light blue skies
the air is moist
 it is okay to be wet here

I can stay for awhile
gazing is time consuming; this is how I will use it
abstract shapes plastered on bodies, lycra is worse
rayon motion across my vision
spandex shields, to meet the quo
 looms have gnashed and whirred, please keep them oiled
for my imagination
so I may enjoy line and form, for all that it is
 distortion is a black swimming suit
 scraps held with taught string, it's not my fault
my interest is entrapment, beginning with the dawn of man
It is not unpleasant, your undulation a thing of beauty
I will not be embarrassed—you brought it, I only saw it
You chose your drape. Your action, an allocation
Revealing teeth, over a cotton strapped shoulder, tilted crescent moon
blue eyes search my face, a barren scape
you descend, slowly walking toward the deep end
It is okay to be wet here

I FALL

into the
grapevine and disappear,
if I don't move they won't find me
for days, The perennial Greenman in a town
where even gunslingers don't survive for
long, so, depart with short notice; no remorse,
passing wall after wall of moss covered limestone
on their way out to the highway, a deeply, rutted mud
filled byway sunken into the forest where one can pass without being seen
until you reach the bridgeless stream, there you will wet your feet or your wheels,
yet the little fish won't mind as you pass, unless you get stuck, then you will be in
their way, impeding their motion and then they will set upon you and do little fish damage
in only the way little fish can, so it is better to go unnoticed in this little town, so, I fall into the English ivy
and disappear, I won't be found for weeks, green on green, the Greenman until the brown of autumn days
you may find my tracks leading out to the path that passes for a road in this county, horseshoes
and wagon wheels littering the sides where Virginia creeper and Poison Sumac seek them out,
skeletal remains of turnip karts and wooden wheel barrows may go unnoticed,
were it not for the tale-tale wooden bones that project up through
the layers of vegetation, pungent, yet attractive to some
who may not be from this town, drawing them in,
only to be a
sad reminder
on their way
out, because,
only I can be
here without
being noticed

IN THE NEIGHBORHOOD OF MY CHILDHOOD

I buried my tender age in the backyard of a house we once shared in your fatherhood. It looked a lot like a dead bird. I regarded it one last time before you forced me to throw the soil of indifference over it. Never knowing I would not be able to find it again. I still remember the brilliant colors of the former. The stagnant, mottled gray of the latter. A once bright and lively eye on the world. Now, glazed with uncertainty. There was a melodic song in the day, right up to the moment. Only imitations, since. I had never killed anything before Time gave me a weapon. Then you showed me how to use it. Against things I loved. Against things that mattered. Against new things that would come after. You were gone in an instant. I could never give it back. It was stuck to me, cold and weighty like cast iron. Frozen to the innocent skin of my childhood.

INTIMATE WITH OLD GROWTH

Light breaks on a dark forested place
Down from fragile lines of yellow, crystalline muted cloud

Find me, on a lonely trail, walled left and right by
century old, bark covered boles concealing ninety-nine rings

They run on ahead, leaving me with expectation
Crowns tipping to reveal visual mysteries

Moving within premeditated earshot
I fall victim to a salvo of creaks and groans

My movement, a goal from the beginning
North or South with ease—sideways with a risk

Because of the scattered bones of the deceased
One's journey is hindered, but not halted

They don't bury their dead

LIFE'S WHISPERING

There is a song being sung
A melodious resonance
An elusive glissade beneath the breeze
Flowing over the open field
Where the long tan grass appears unmoved
Tis my Mother's mantra
Enhancing the pulse of life blood in a certain type of heart
It becomes a tattoo that rolls out beyond the limits of our vision
Benefiting our restless feet
Where no single square foot of ground will ever be enough
The pines will capture and mimic
In their company, a sky song
In my isolation, a memory of a secret sirens lullaby

LONELINESS

Loneliness comes—
A shadowy figure on dark and heavy steed.
Faceless, it rends the cool mist
swirling over the verdant lawn that is your illusion.
The one you endeavored so, to create and keep,
void of mindful effort.
A barrier to the jagged rock and brazen thorn.
Forever itinerate, its presence passes into the distance
its power in its visage.
Yet, the further you can see,
the longer you shall ache.

MEMORIES CASCADE LIKE WATER DOWN MY DAY

```
E      e
M      m
O  C     o
R      a     r
I  L  s     i
E  i  c       e
S  W  k   a     s
       a     e     d
C       t         e
A  D  e
S     o       r
C  M  w
A    y    n
D  D
E  a
     y
L
I  A
K
E     B
        a
W  B  b
A  r   b
T  O  o   l
E  f  o   i
R  C     k   n
        a       g
D  C    c
```

O   o   o
W   F g   p
N   l n   h
     D o i   o
M   i a   t n
Y   s t   i   i
       t i   o c
D   a n   n
A   n   g,
Y   t

               By and by, I ride the swells
       of an ocean of regret   Treading the aqueous depths
                            of profound images
                                 Soon I grow
                                     tired
                       Exhausted, I drown
                         in my own
                     reflection

MORNING

She arrives with the dawning glow
Clad in her lucent gown of mist
Every red tea rose, arbor bound
Will rejoice in petals kissed

Heralded by the Phoebe bold
Into my chamber, brash not shy
Filling the room with pleasant light
She embraces me where I lie

Not unlike the resplendent buds
She is kissing each lidded eye
Her warmth it fills my quiet space
I receive her with grateful sigh

She lies with me, her touch is kind
I respond to her gentle way
Yet, I depart my morning love
So I may meet my friend, the day

NOT A POT OF GOLD, HOWEVER...

I travel to many places
One of them—
a spot where a rainbow
rests upon the earth

It does no harm to be there
Colors don't do damage
It can just—be there
Bestowing perspectives

Lingering in its spectrum
I too can just rest there
With other human beings
touching me—without ever touching me

Reminding me
of a liveliness I can't find
anywhere else outside
that many hued phenomenon

A singular jauntiness
A painless jollity
A saturating sense of cheer
Glee

I am not one of them
Yet—I am
Color does no damage

ON THE SUBJECT OF GIRLS CRYING IN THE BACKSEATS OF CARS

She cried in the car, in the back seat, by herself, except for the dog
We didn't know why, she didn't want to share, just out of the blue
The dog licked at black vinyl, doing away with tattle-tale tears
We stood outside, staring through windows, perplexed at motives
Frowning at the little white terrier, who did not weep, because…
Dogs do not shed tears, in the backseats of cars, with girls

ONCE, A LONG TIME AGO

A.J. Downing wrote a book, The Architecture of Country Houses
In it you will find a drawing of an 1850's cottage
It is where I am going to go live someday,
having had enough of modern life

A place where penciled gothic spires rise against the clouds,
those M shaped birds, flying
Where, a dozen or so, two-dimensional woodcut printed trees are
placed
strategically upon my pretend lawn

The 19th century sun always shining lazily
even when the book is closed
It is quiet, and a carelessly drawn Hudson river
flows in the background

Hollow sheep graze its grassless banks
next to a faceless fisherman
whose cane pole swings a fish outline
against parchment water

He is waving to the voluptuous and also faceless woman
whose outline stands on the balcony of my house
She waves back with her ridiculously long arm
her dress blowing in the nonexistent wind

All I will have to do is take my pen and draw myself into that
lovely scene,
hoping they will not be too surprised with my unexpected arrival

Lounging on the gingerbread endowed arcade porch,
they will invite me in for tea

We will converse about good Victorian architecture
and how it will cure all the ills of the world
Yet before I leave this place for my new pastoral life
with pen in hand, I will give them faces

ONLY I

I play on the open plain in the dark.

Playing a worthless game of Marco polo.
Playing with a firefly.
Playing a pan flute.
Playing with the thought of going to some place more populated.
Playing with myself.

There is no light out here on a moonless night.
There are no clouds.
There is no voice to be heard, only the coyote call.
There is the moaning of a breeze to haunt my ear.

A desire to move.

I move toward the darker shadows that rise up in the distance.
I move toward a disposition that is strangely familiar.
I move my finger to the illumination button on my watch.

2:00am.

The stars twinkle in an ink blue bowl.
The stars have the company of hurtling UFO that streak between
them, leaving the question.
The stars don't care if I am bitten by a warmth seeking serpent.

The stars make me lonely.

Only for the solitude.
Only for the life that exists in my head.
Only I can tell you what it is like for me.

Only I

PINNACLE AT 25

What is offered in a life stolen?
It is more about what we need.
You are bonded by age six
Ensnared by a carefully constructed scaffold
of a solidly welded family unit.
Your time wasted by those with judicious intent

This will save you from:
Choking
Falling down the stairs
Getting hit by a car
Attacked by an animal
Poison

Play on the sidewalk, not in the street
In the back garden, not in the alley
Not in a parking lot
Not in a canyon,
or a dark wood

You are old by age twelve,
and reined in by sixteen
Your freedom arrives two years later
You now have seven years to make up for lost time
Twenty five—the summit
In real life there is no room for perfection.

REPOSE

I lay along a line of vague wakefulness
As straight as I can make myself
If only I could widen out…
Stabilizing by becoming a vast area, resting
A thin alternative, coating a flat plane
finding a kind of balance for the sake of it
I am entwining with a 200-thread count
Passing through the veil with the least resistance
I come together on the other side
Over there I am different
Yet—the same

RESISTANCE

Sometimes I need to grab a hold on something
Maybe so I won't slip away into the river
that is time
To slow things down
I may flip and flop, sidling back and forth
Against a human crafted current of ticking—tocking
Stretched to my limits, I release my hold
Fearful
I plunge my hands into nature's flotsam to find
a stable root on which to cling
Only for a minute

ROWING AS A SOULTION

I moved around the attic in my rowboat. Floating past grandma's time worn trunk of misapprehensions. Grandpa's pipe rack. Oarlocks squeaking in time with my arduous breathing. Rowing is hard work when suspended in the nostalgic waters of an upper room. My once sturdy hull, drags across stacks of submerged photo albums. The face of my pitiless aunt, glowering from the open pages of Vol. 2. The accepting look of her sister who I had suckled on day one. My forward motion temporarily blocked by my father's hat and cane, precariously slung on a dilapidated hall tree, stubbornly pushed aside. My exertion noted. My paddle strikes a column that bears the roof, giving me the leverage I need to move away. I need to move away. From the accusing eyes of perfect porcelain doll faces. The small waves of my motion dashing them against the exposed studs of my internal life. I am expected to save them all. There just isn't enough room in my boat. I lay back, resting my oars as I bump down the progressive waters of the staircase. I find myself grinning at the smiling portraits of my wife and children as I scuttle past. Passing under the 'Freedom!' quote on the rustic plank hung above the door, I swirl out onto the veranda of yet another year.

SO SIMPLE

It was as simple as a tree top
Where I contrast the pinnacle
Only connecting at sunset
Posterior to the wind

I am then, the zenith
An apex of rumination
It is—where it ends
From the bottom—up

But only for that day
The night a treacherous decent
Fear of the bent and broken
Earthbound until the dawn

Where it starts
My mind, a mirror
Turned toward the past
It was as simple as a tree top

SOJOURNERS BONE YARD

a desert born of countless hour glasses
smashed upon the time worn bedrock of a naked earth
saguaro sentinels reach their arms to the sky
warning us away from barrel cactus landmines
scattered throughout passive long grass
needle covered dwarves bristling

prickly pear extend hand like paddles
as if to welcome the interloper to their fruit
a deceptive posture to lure the unsuspecting
to experience its hair like prickles, leaving
victims to writhe in the century old dust
a one act play under the spotlight of a glaring sun

intrude at your own risk its
a one way ticket to the end
in a waterless world
were pit vipers slither and toads bear horns
blood spewing from their eyes as
beaded lizards bask—indifferent to your demise

THE ASHES OF YOUR FACE

Your face I will not forget in a forest where pencil thin poplars gain the sky, cloud laden, heavy in its pregnancy of mist and shadowy fringe. The weeping brought me to where I could see you, walking, stumbling, your long dark dress perused by cocklebur, blackberry and wild rose. Against grey trunks and fluttering tree born saffron, your hue contrary. I moved to where you are, to face your picture of seemingly despair. Hair muted yellow, slashed to within a poppy seed of your shoulders, lips quivering, in your blue eyes the history of your life. Hieroglyphs I could not decipher. The tears mapping your face, rolling though white ash. In your hand, a small twig blackened. Putting your birch to my blouse, you scribed the shield knot. Charcoal dust cascaded, driven by a delicate breeze to begrime bare feet. Chafed, manifesting an arduous journey. Your breasts heaved beneath tattered brocade to beget a pensive sigh. A pale hand through soiled lace cupped my cheek. You kissed me soft but meteoric. Without words you moved away. Bending to sob, your back a barren veldt of naught. Lamenting words I do not know, the hedgerow folded you in. I taste your ashes upon my lips. Affirmation.

THE EXISTENCE MAZE, SHARP EDGED, TINED TOPPED, AND KEEN

I awake
Becoming aware of the existence maze
Back again from some place I can't put my finger on
My Mother Nature sees to it I don't wander too far
While living, keeping me from climbing over life's hedges
tine topped and keen, sharp edged and agonizing
Pain filled to remind us that we are alive

THE HOPELESS ROMANTIC

I am sorry

I don't love you
I don't love your face
I don't love your body
Or any part of it

I don't love cars
I don't love clothes
I don't love money
Or anything, of a material nature

I don't love my methods
I don't love my privilege
I don't love my accolades
And surely not, my pride

Yet, if you must know…

I love the wind as it stirs the world
I love the trees who shade and shed
I love the dew laden grass upon the hill
And the sea, the stars, the gentle rain

I love the sun that lights my path
I love the moon on my lonely nights
I love the pain that reminds me that I'm alive
And the sadness that unveils my frailty

I love the empathy I see in your deeds
I love the kindness I see in your faces
I love the warmth I feel in your hands
And your unconditional acceptance, when I fall

But, most of all—I love, love

X

It seems,
humans need to put meaning to everything
It is as if they feel unattached
Alien to the natural world
It is as if by doing so
there can be a claim of contribution
It is as if they long to touch, but can't
Truly
X
So, certain
humans need to understand
Your body is just your vessel
So the true you may move freely to experience
Your face is just, how we recognize you
so you may be renowned,
however, your self is within,
Exceptionally